Dear Taryn,

To celebrate your dedication ceremony, Oct 13/13.

love,

Bestemor & Bestefa

Presented to

_____

By

_____

On

_____

For my daughter, Amanda Bloom Briggs.
–JKB

To Sandy, my cousin (but more like my sister), and Cody, her son.
–SB

ZONDERKIDZ

Bible Promises for God's Precious Princess
Copyright © 2013 Zondervan
Illustrations © 2013 by Sheila Bailey

Requests for information should be addressed to:

Zondervan, 5300 Patterson Ave. SE, Grand Rapids, Michigan 49530

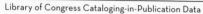

Library of Congress Cataloging-in-Publication Data

Bloom, Jean Kavich.
    Bible promises for God's precious princess / Jean Kavich Bloom.
      p. cm.
    ISBN 978-0-310-72367-7
      1. God (Christianity)—Promises—Juvenile literature. 2. Girls—Religious
life—Juvenile literature. 3. Girls—Conduct of life—Juvenile literature. 4.
Christian children—Religious life—Juvenile literature 5. Christian children—
Conduct of life—Juvenile literature. 6. Bible—Indexes—Juvenile literature.
I. Title.
BS680.P68B56 2013
242'.62—dc23
                                                                2012027531

Editor: Mary Hassinger
Design and art direction: Kris Nelson

Printed in China

12 13 14 15 16 /DSC/ 22 21 20 19 18 17 16 15 14 13 12 11 10 9 8 7 6 5 4 3 2 1

BIBLE PROMISES FOR
God's
Precious
Princess

WRITTEN BY JEAN KAVICH BLOOM
ILLUSTRATED BY SHEILA BAILEY

ZONDERkidz

ZONDERVAN.com/
AUTHORTRACKER
follow your favorite authors

God shows his wonderfu

Table of Contents

page

promises through his ...

You show you trust God

__ Brave	__ Friendly
__ Careful	__ Generous
__ Caring	__ Gentle
__ Celebrating	__ Giving
__ Cheerful	__ God's Child
__ Compassionate	__ Good to Your Friends
__ Considerate	__ Growing
__ Counting Your Blessings	__ Helpful
__ Dancing	__ Humble
__ Doing the Right Thing	__ Joyful
__ Doing Your Best	__ Kind
__ Encouraged	__ Learning
__ Faithful	__ Listening
__ Following Jesus	__ Loving
__ Forgiving	__ Obedient

promises when you are ...

__ Patient	__ Sharing
__ Peacemaking	__ Showing His Ways
__ Persevering	__ Showing Mercy
__ Pleasant	__ Showing Self-Control
__ Pleasing God	__ Slow to Anger
__ Power-Filled	__ Sorry
__ Praising God	__ Strong
__ Praying	__ Thankful
__ Pure	__ Trusting
__ Resisting Temptation	__ Trustworthy
__ Responsible	__ Truthful
__ Resting	__ Understanding
__ Seeking God's Help	__ Watching Your Words
__ Serving God	__ Wise
__ Serving Others	__ Working

The Bible is God's Word.

The books in it were written so you can
learn what God is like and what promises
he has made. Everything in the Bible is
absolutely true. God does not lie!

God isn't a mere man. He can't lie. He isn't a human being.
He doesn't change his mind. He speaks, and then he acts.
He makes a promise, and then he keeps it.

Numbers 23:19

We know that Scripture is always true.

John 10:35

God has breathed life into all of Scripture.
It is useful for teaching us what is true.

2 Timothy 3:16

I Trust God's Promise

Put your hand on your Bible and say, "God always tells the truth!" Now when you hear about his promises from the Bible, you will remember why you can trust everything God says.

God's Bible

Look at what these verses

from the Bible tell you. God promises his
Word is like the food we need to live.
But it's not only true; it will last forever.
So a girl like you can believe it!

Jesus answered, "It is written, 'Man doesn't live only on bread.
He also lives on every word that comes from the mouth
of God.'"

Matthew 4:4

The grass dries up. The flowers fall to the ground. But what
our God says will stand forever.

Isaiah 40:8

(Jesus said) "Heaven and earth will pass away. But my words
will never pass away."

Matthew 24:35

I Trust God's Promise

Will your favorite foods last forever? No! But God's Word does. Find or draw a picture of one of your favorite foods. Then draw a Bible by it to remind you of God's promise about his Word—that it will last forever.

God's Bible

God told the Bible writers

to only say what is true. So you can
believe God's prophets knew all about
his promises about Jesus long, long before
Jesus came to earth.

But God had given a promise through all the prophets. And
this is how he has made his promise come true. He said that
his Christ would suffer.

Acts 3:18

He promised the good news long ago. He announced it
through his prophets in the Holy Scriptures.

Romans 1:2

Jesus said to them, "This is what I told you while I was still
with you. Everything written about me must happen."

Luke 24:44

I Trust God's Promise

God promised everything about Jesus in the Bible is true. Nothing is made up. Tell a story you know about Jesus. Aren't God's true stories the best stories ever?!

God's Bible

In his Bible, God promises
that hearing and obeying his Word
will help you love him, live for him, and
learn how to do good. Jesus said you are
blessed when you obey God's Word!

(Jesus said) "... Blessed are those who hear
God's word and obey it."

Luke 11:28

But if anyone obeys God's word,
then God's love is truly made complete in that person.

1 John 2:5

By using Scripture, a man of God can be
completely prepared to do every good thing.

2 Timothy 3:17

I Trust God's Promise

Where do you hear God's Word? At home? At church? On the playground? Learn what Jesus said in Luke 11:28 by heart. Say it every day this week to help you remember to hear and obey God's Word.

God's Blessings

A blessing is like a good gift from God,
something you need or even want. God loves you
so much that he promises you many blessings
as you love and serve him! Do you think
God's blessings are too many to count?

God is able to shower all kinds of blessings on you. In all things and
at all times you will have everything you need.

2 Corinthians 9:8

Lord and King, you are God! Your words can be trusted. You have
promised many good things to me.

2 Samuel 7:28

The Lord always does what is right. So he loves it when people do
what is fair. Those who are honest will enjoy his blessing.

Psalm 11:7

I Trust God's Promise

Can you think of blessings God has given you? Count as many as you can—even write them down! Now thank him and praise him for his wonderful promise to bless you.

God's
Blessings

Did you know

God promises blessings when you trust his ways
and do what is right? The good feeling you get
when you are pleasing God is a blessing!
Isn't that amazing for a girl to know? Yes!

Blessed is the man who trusts in the Lord.

Psalm 40:4

Blessed are those who are hungry and thirsty for what is right.

Matthew 5:6

(God said) "I will bless any man who trusts in me.
I will show my favor to the one who depends on me."

Jeremiah 17:7

I Trust God's Promise

Guess what? God can help you bless others! Ask him what good thing he wants you to do for someone today. Maybe you can help your teacher, play ball with a classmate, or share a treat with a friend. You are a blessing.

God's Blessings

God promises blessings

when you do good works. Sometimes doing good works is easy and sometimes it is hard. But God will bless you for all the good works you do. And he'll help you too!

The Lord blesses anyone who does good.

Proverbs 12:2

Your work will give you what you need.
Blessings and good things will come to you.

Psalm 128:2

(Jesus said) "But love your enemies. Do good to them.
Lend to them without expecting to get anything back.
Then you will receive a lot in return."

Luke 6:35

I Trust God's Promise

God wants you to help others who aren't always very nice to you. Sometimes that is hard! Ask him to help you think of a good thing to do for someone like that today. Then they will know God too!

God's Care

God cares for everything he has made:

the earth, the animals, people, and you!

That's because he loves what he makes.

Even if you are tempted to think he doesn't care,

God promises that he does—and will forever.

The Lord is good to all.
He shows deep concern for everything he has made.

Psalm 145:9

His loving concern never fails.

Lamentations 3:22

"… I will show you my loving concern.
My faithful love will continue forever," says the Lord.

Isaiah 54:8

I Trust God's Promise

Can you draw or write down ten animals?
Try it! Think about how much God loves the
animals and then think about ways people care
for animals too. (Hint: Being gentle.)

God's Care

Are you afraid sometimes?

God promises to hear you when you call him.
If you trust God, he will take good care of you
and always be with you. You can depend on that!

When I'm in trouble, I will call out to you.
And you will answer me.

Psalm 86:7

The Lord is good.
When people are in trouble, they can go to him for safety.
He takes good care of those who trust in him.

Nahum 1:7

"Be strong and brave. Do not be terrified . . .
I am the Lord your God. I will be with you
everywhere you go."

Joshua 1:9

I Trust God's Promise

Tell God what scares you. Ask him to help you to be brave no matter where you go—school, a friend's house, or even the beach. Thank God for caring about your fears.

God's Care

God promises to bless you

when you do right. He promises to keep you safe and listen to you when you tell him about your worries. God really cares about you— just like a shepherd scoops up his sheep to love and care for them!

Lord, you bless those who do what is right.
Like a shield, your loving care keeps them safe.
Psalm 5:12

Turn all your worries over to him. He cares about you.
1 Peter 5:7

He takes care of his flock like a shepherd.
He gathers the lambs in his arms.
He carries them close to his heart.
Isaiah 40:11

I Trust God's Promise

Have you seen a lamb at a zoo or on TV?
Maybe a zookeeper took care of it. But in
some parts of the world, a shepherd cares
for sheep. Explain how that is like the way
Jesus cares for you.

God's Care

God promises to care for you

because he loves you. He gives you food,
warmth, light, rest, and even rain.
And God will comfort all those who are sad and
in need: women, men, boys—and girls like you.

As long as the earth lasts, there will always be a time to plant
and a time to gather the crops. As long as the earth lasts,
there … will always be summer and winter, day and night.

Genesis 8:22

He sends rain in the fall and the spring. He promises us
that the harvest will come at the same time each year.

Jeremiah 5:24

The Lord will comfort his people. He will show
his tender love to those who are suffering.

Isaiah 49:13

I Trust God's Promise

God wants you to comfort someone who is sad or in trouble. Ask a grown-up about a way you can help someone in need, even someone you don't know from church. Then do it! God wants you to be like him this way.

God's Children

God promises you can be a daughter
in his family. Jesus died for you!
And God's Holy Spirit chooses you!
What a promise your heavenly Father gives you!
Celebrate!

So he decided long ago to adopt us as his children.
He did it because of what Jesus Christ has done.
It pleased God to do it.

Ephesians 1:5

As his children, we will receive all that he has for us.

Romans 8:17

He put his Spirit in our hearts and marked us as his own.
We can now be sure that he will give us
everything he promised us.

2 Corinthians 1:22

I Trust God's Promise

What do you do when you celebrate something? Play music? Sing? Dance? Celebrate now if you are where it is okay to make some noise. You are God's daughter—and that's a wonderful thing!

God's Correction

God says you will learn

what is right when you follow his directions.
If you disobey, he will correct you.
But God promises to protect and
bless you no matter what—especially
when you obey and do right!

Blessed is the person God corrects.

Job 5:17

"I am the Lord your God. I teach you what is best for you.
I direct you in the way you should go."

Isaiah 48:17

Blessed are those who obey the law.

Proverbs 29:18

I Trust God's Promise

If a driver doesn't follow road signs that tell him to stop, he might get in trouble or have an accident. Tell three things God says to "STOP!" so you won't get hurt.
(Hint: Lying.)

God's Correction

God promises that

even when he corrects you he is blessing you.
That's because serving God and doing right will
give you life—a happy, restful life in him!

The training that corrects you leads to life.

Proverbs 6:23

Lord, blessed is the man you correct.
Blessed is the person you teach from your law.

Psalm 94:12

(Jesus said) "Become my servants and learn from me.
I am gentle and free of pride. You will find rest for your souls."

Matthew 11:29

I Trust God's Promise

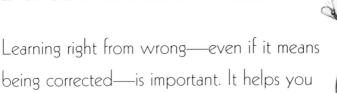

Learning right from wrong—even if it means being corrected—is important. It helps you live a life that pleases God. Name three good things that happen when you do right. (Hint: You are blessed.)

God's Covenants

Sometimes God makes an agreement
called a covenant—like when he promised
Noah safety if he built a boat.
God's covenant with you promises
life with him forever if you believe in Jesus!

The Lord (said to Abram) "... Count the stars, if you can ...
That is how many children you will have" ...
The Lord made a covenant with Abram. He said,
"I am giving this land to your children after you ...
All of that will happen because you have obeyed me."

Genesis 15:4–5; 18

(God said) "Here is my covenant that I am making with you.
The waters of a flood will never destroy all life again."

Genesis 9:11

(Jesus) is the go-between of a new covenant.

Hebrews 12:24

I Trust God's Promise

Try to answer some questions about Noah's story (GEN. 6–9): Was Noah's family on the boat? Did he gather only one of each animal? What did God put in the sky after the flood—and why?

God's Creations

God's creation is a promise.

Everything on earth and in heaven shows
he really is the one, true, forever God.
And if God created everything and everyone,
that means he created a girl who is ... you!

The Lord is the God who lives forever.
He created everything on earth.

Isaiah 40:28

You are the one and only Lord. You made the heavens ...
You created all of the stars in the sky. You created the earth
and everything that is on it.

Nehemiah 9:6

Ever since the world was created it has been possible to see
the qualities of God that are not seen ... about the fact that he
is God. Those things can be seen in what he has made.

Romans 1:20

I Trust God's Promise

Find three things God created. Now find
a photo of or draw a picture of … you!
Thank God—the one, true God—right now
for creating and loving wonderful you.

God's Creations

God is so creative!

He promises you a new life and makes
wonderful plans for you because he made you and
loves you! You are like a new girl when you follow
God's plan—a girl with a new heart for God.

Anyone who believes in Christ is a new creation.
The old is gone! The new has come!

2 Corinthians 5:17

"I know the plans I have for you," announces the Lord.
"I want you to enjoy success. I do not plan to harm you.
I will give you hope for the years to come."

Jeremiah 29:11

The Lord is faithful and will keep all of his promises.
He is loving toward everything he has made.

Psalm 145:13

I Trust God's Promise

Draw a heart and print "GOD MADE ME!" on it. Put it where you can see it each morning so you don't forget God has promised to always love you. He has good plans for your life.

GOD MADE ME

God's Faithfulness

God promises that he will be faithful

to us, love us, and be good to us forever.
He is there for us when we love and obey him—
and when we need his forgiveness.
Now that's being faithful!

He is the faithful God. He keeps his covenant
for all time to come. He keeps it with those who
love him and obey his commands.

Deuteronomy 7:9

Give thanks to the Lord, because he is good.
His faithful love continues forever.

1 Chronicles 16:34

But God is faithful and fair.
If we admit that we have sinned, he will forgive us our sins.
He will forgive every wrong thing we have done.

1 John 1:9

I Trust God's Promise

God wants you to be faithful to him too.
He wants to be able to depend on you to
do good. Is there one thing you can do
every day for someone you love so they
can depend on you? Tell God what it is
and do it!

God's Faithfulness

Here are three ways God shows
his promise to be faithful: he will never change
like shadows do, he will help you resist
temptation to do wrong, and he has
chosen you to be with his Son, Jesus.
You can depend on all that!

Every good and perfect gift is from God. It comes down from
the Father ... He does not change like shadows that move.

James 1:17

God is faithful ... when you are tempted, God will
give you a way out so that you can stand up under it.

1 Corinthians 10:13

God is faithful. He has chosen you to share life
with his Son, Jesus Christ our Lord.

1 Corinthians 1:9

I Trust God's Promise

Sometimes someone changes and disappoints you—as if they changed a puzzle piece so you can't make the same picture anymore. Work or make a puzzle to remind you God never changes.

God's Followers

God shows his promises through his

followers in the Bible like Paul and Peter.
When they preached and shared, they taught
about his promises. They taught about God's promise
to forgive so that others would follow him too.

I, Paul, am writing this letter. I am an apostle of Christ Jesus
just as God planned. He sent me to tell about
the promise of life that is found in Christ Jesus.

2 Timothy 1:1

Peter (said), "All of you must turn away from your sins and
be baptized in the name of Jesus Christ. Then your sins will be
forgiven. You will receive the gift of the Holy Spirit.
The promise is for you and your children."

Acts 2:38–39

(God said) "(If) they pray and look to me … and they turn from
their evil ways, then I will listen to them from heaven. I will
forgive their sin."

2 Chronicles 7:14

I Trust God's Promise

PAUL

Did you ever play Follow the Leader
or Simon Says? Being a good follower is
important sometimes, and especially when
you follow God. Name three ways followers
did what God said to do. (Hint: Prayed.)

God's Followers

Jesus had many followers

in the Bible—followers like John, to whom
God sent special visions, and Lydia, who
worshiped God. God promised that even boys
and girls—like you!—will follow and praise Jesus.

John gives witness to everything he saw …
God's word and what Jesus Christ has said.

Revelation 1:2

(Lydia's) business was selling purple cloth.
She was a worshiper of God.

Acts 16:14

"Do you hear what these children are saying?" they asked him.
"Yes," replied Jesus. "Haven't you ever read about it in Scripture?
It says, 'You have made sure that children and infants praise you.'"

Matthew 21:16

I Trust God's Promise

You might follow people when you think they are special. But sometimes you can make a mistake and follow someone who makes bad choices. Tell why you think it is safe to ALWAYS follow Jesus.

God's Forgiveness

God promises to forgive you

when you are sorry for doing wrong.
Be sincere and ask God for his forgiveness.
Then God promises even more! He will not keep
track of your sins. He will wipe them away—
and not remember them!

God is faithful and fair.
If we admit that we have sinned, he will forgive us our sins.

1 John 1:9

(God said) "I am the one who wipes out your lawless acts.
I do it because of who I am.
I will not remember your sins anymore."

Isaiah 43:25

Blessed is the man whose sin the Lord
never counts against him.

Romans 4:8

I Trust God's Promise

Write down or draw about a bad choice you
have made. Now, erase what's on the paper
and throw it away. That's how God forgives
your sins when you are sorry. He forgives
and forgets.

God's Forgiveness

God promises you can come to him without being afraid to ask for his forgiveness. He wants you to be forgiving too. And guess what else? It may be hard for us to keep from getting angry with others, but it is not hard for God!

"I am the Lord. I am slow to get angry. I am full of love. I forgive those who sin."

Numbers 14:18

Through him and through faith in him we can approach God. We can come to him freely. We can come without fear.

Ephesians 3:12

(Jesus said) "Forgive anyone you have anything against. Then your Father in heaven will forgive your sins."

Mark 11:25–26

I Trust God's Promise

Here's one way to keep from being mean or disrespectful: Count to ten before you open your mouth to say something whenever you are upset. Try it! Jesus will help you.

God's Gifts

Every gift is from God.

He promises that you can ask for anything if you stay close to Jesus and ask in Jesus' name. If God thinks it is best for you, he will give it to you!

God gives life to everything.

1 Timothy 6:13

(Jesus said) "If you remain joined to me and my words remain in you, ask for anything you wish. And it will be given to you."

John 15:7

(Jesus said) "And I will do anything you ask in my name. Then the Son will bring glory to the Father. You may ask me for anything in my name. I will do it."

John 14:13–14

I Trust God's Promise

God knows when it is not best for you to
have what you want when you want it.
He loves you enough to say "no" or "wait."
Thank him for caring so much about you—
even when his
answers are hard
to understand.

God's Gifts

God promises the very best gift of all —
a forever life with him in heaven.
If you accept Jesus and ask God
to forgive your sins, someday you will live
like a princess with God, the King of heaven!

God gives you the gift of eternal life
because of what Christ Jesus our Lord has done.

Romans 6:23

Now there is a crown waiting for me.
It is given to those who are right with God.

2 Timothy 4:8

God is King … he establishes peace
in the highest parts of heaven.

Job 25:2

I Trust God's Promise

Do you like to pretend you are a princess?
You don't even have to pretend. You are a
princess to God when you belong to him.
Close your eyes and imagine being his
princess forever. Then stand up and twirl!

God's Gift of New Life

Jesus came to die for your sins

and save you. It was what God promised he
would do. Only Jesus can save you.
Jesus is the promise!

Christ has been raised from the dead by the Father's glory.
And like Christ we also can live a new life.

Romans 6:4

He saved us. It wasn't because of the good things
we had done. It was because of his mercy.
He saved us by washing away our sins.

Titus 3:5

God's grace has saved you because of your faith in Christ.
Your salvation doesn't come from anything you do.
It is God's gift.

Ephesians 2:8

I Trust God's Promise

You try to be a very good girl. That's good!
But no one is perfect. That is why you
can be happy God sent Jesus to save
you, even if you are not perfect. Say,
"Thank you, Jesus!"

God's Gift of New Life

If we love Jesus, we have new life
even when we are still on earth. Jesus said
it's like being born again. You are a growing girl,
not a baby. But God promises that
Jesus can make you like new in your spirit.

God chose to give us new birth through the message of truth.

James 1:18

God gave you new life together with Christ.
He forgave us all of our sins.

Colossians 2:13

He has given us new birth …
It is a gift that can never be destroyed …
It is kept in heaven for you.

1 Peter 1:4

I Trust God's Promise

Did you ever get to help take care of baby animals? You have to be very gentle with them. You are gentle on the inside when Jesus' spirit lives inside you. Think of one way you can be gentle with someone today.

God's Goodness

Because he loves you,
God promises to be good to you—
especially when you show your love for him.
You are a girl who has dreams in her heart.
If you love God, he will pay
special attention to those dreams.

The Lord is good to those who put their hope in him.
He is good to those who look to him.

Lamentations 3:25

The Lord is good. His faithful love continues forever.
It will last for all time to come.

Psalm 100:5

Find your delight in the Lord.
Then he will give you everything your heart really wants.

Psalm 37:4

I Trust God's Promise

What are your dreams? To be a ballerina or a scientist? To travel the world? To someday be a mom? Make a list and ask God to pay attention to your dreams. When you love him, he wants to give you what your heart really wants, if it is good for you.

God's Goodness

God promises to be good to you

by helping you understand his ways. You can trust him to teach you what is best and make your godly ways and honest life shine for him.

Do not depend on your own understanding.
In all your ways remember him. Then he will make
your paths smooth and straight.

Proverbs 3:5–6

"I am the Lord your God. I teach you what is best for you.
I direct you in the way you should go."

Isaiah 48:17

Commit your life to the Lord. Here is what he will do if you
trust in him. He will make your godly ways shine like the dawn.
He will make your honest life shine like the sun at noon.

Psalm 37:5–6

I Trust God's Promise

When you learn God's ways, you can shine
for him. Practice putting a big, shiny smile
on your face. If someone asks you why
you are smiling, tell them it is because
God is so good!

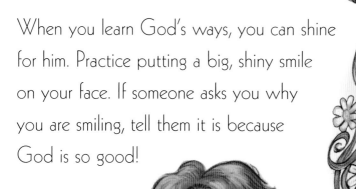

God's Goodness

Jesus promises not to leave you
when you are tired of problems or of doing
wrong. He gives you rest, helps you work things
out, and forgives you as you forgive others.
He understands when you are tired!
Think how he felt when he carried his cross!

(Jesus said) "Come to me, all of you who are tired
and are carrying heavy loads. I will give you rest."

Matthew 11:28

We know that in all things God works for
the good of those who love him.

Romans 8:28

(Jesus said) "If you do not judge others, then you will not be
judged. If you do not find others guilty, then you will not be
found guilty. Forgive, and you will be forgiven."

Luke 6:37

I Trust God's Promise

Hard things can make you feel sad, tired, or even scared. If you are thinking of something like that now, tell God about it. Remember, he is working for good.

God's Grace

Grace means that God is good

to you even if you don't deserve it. He promises
to give forgiveness and many other blessings too!

Those who receive the rich supply of God's grace will rule
with Christ in his kingdom. They have received God's gift
and have been made right with him.

Romans 5:17

God has saved us … It wasn't because of anything we have
done. It was because of his own purpose and grace.
Through Christ Jesus, God gave us that grace
even before time began.

2 Timothy 1:9

We have all received one blessing after another.
God's grace is not limited.

John 1:16

I Trust God's Promise

God wants you to show grace to others,
even if they don't deserve it. Can you think of
people who aren't very nice to you? Be nice
to them the next time you see them. God will
help you and bless you.

When God shows you grace,

he gives you mercy. That means he doesn't
punish you for sins like you might deserve.
God promises to forgive you and
give you eternal life instead. He is a King
waiting on his throne to give you grace!

God the Father and Jesus Christ his Son
will give you grace, mercy and peace.
Those blessings will be with us because we love the truth.
2 John 1:3

The mercy of our Lord Jesus Christ will bring you eternal life.
Jude 1:21

Let us boldly approach the throne of grace.
Then we will receive mercy.

Hebrews 4:16

I Trust God's Promise

Sometimes it seems like it would be all right to get even with someone for being mean. But why does God think that is not the right idea? (Hint: Ask yourself what Jesus would do.)

God's Home in Heaven

God promised Jesus would
give people the chance to be with him in heaven.
If you belong to Jesus, your name is already
written down in heaven to say that
will be your home someday.

Faith and understanding rest on the hope of eternal life.
Before time began, God promised to give that life.
And he does not lie.

Titus 1:2

God's people share in what belongs to his Son.
Their names are written in heaven.

Hebrews 12:23

We know that God raised the Lord Jesus from the dead.
And he will also raise us up with Jesus.
He will bring us with you to God in heaven.

2 Corinthians 4:14

I Trust God's Promise

Write your name on some paper. Put it on the refrigerator to remind yourself that if you belong to Jesus, your name is already written down in heaven. You can live there someday.

God's Home in Heaven

Jesus promises

he'll take you to heaven someday, if you belong
to him. And God promises there is no pain or
sadness in heaven. Sometimes a girl is sad and
needs to cry on earth, but not in heaven!

(Jesus said) … "I will come back. And I will take you to be with
me. Then you will also be where I am."

John 14:3

He will bring you into his heavenly glory without any fault.
He will bring you there with great joy.

Jude 1:24

He will wipe away every tear from their eyes.
There will be no more death or sadness.
There will be no more crying or pain.

Revelation 21:4

I Trust God's Promise

It's hard to always be happy on earth.
Sometimes bad things happen. But someday
when you live in heaven, you'll have no more
sadness! Frown and then smile. Then do it
again. Which do you like best?

God's Holy Spirit

God promised to send his Holy Spirit

when Jesus returned to heaven. And he did—to
his followers on earth so they could have God's
love in their hearts and help do his work.
The Holy Spirit is a friend!

(Jesus said) "But the Father will send the Friend in my name to
help you. The Friend is the Holy Spirit. He will teach you all
things. He will remind you of everything I have said to you."

John 14:26

Jesus has been given a place of honor at the right hand of God.
He has received the Holy Spirit from the Father.
This is what God had promised.

Acts 2:33

God has poured his love into our hearts. He did it through the
Holy Spirit, whom he has given to us.

Romans 5:5

I Trust God's Promise

Do you have a friend who helps you? Name one thing you can do for that friend to show your love. Then thank God for your friend and for the Holy Spirit, who helps you know God's ways.

God's
Holy Spirit

The Holy Spirit is with those

who trust God. God promises that his Spirit
speaks God's words to you, gives you a life
for God, and helps you to know what to say
for God. You can really smile about that!

The One whom God has sent speaks God's words.
God gives the Holy Spirit without limit.

John 3:34

The Holy Spirit gives life …
The words I have spoken to you are from the Spirit.
They give life.

John 6:63

"The Holy Spirit will teach you at that time
what you should say."

Luke 12:12

I Trust God's Promise

Learn Luke 12:12 and say it every day this week. That will remind you that the Holy Spirit will help you when you don't know what to say.

God's Joy

Did you know you can have joy in your heart and be glad even if you sometimes feel unhappy? That's because God promises you can know in your heart that he has forgiven you and that you belong to him no matter what happens.

Let me hear you say, "Your sins are forgiven."
That will bring me joy and gladness.

Psalm 51:8

Always be joyful because you belong to the Lord.

Philippians 4:4

I will be glad and full of joy because of you.

Psalm 9:2

I Trust God's Promise

It can be hard to feel joyful when you have unhappy thoughts. But if you act joyful, you can start to feel joyful. Smile and sing a joyful song about how God loves you. God will give you joy.

God's Joy

Jesus knows how you feel

when you are sick or hurt. But even then God promises you joy in your heart. Ask others to pray for God to give you comfort and make you well when you need it—and for his joy too!

A man's cheerful heart gives him strength when he is sick.

Proverbs 18:14

A large crowd of people followed (Jesus).
They had seen the miraculous signs he had done
on those who were sick.

John 6:2

I was very worried.
But your comfort brought joy to my heart.

Psalm 94:19

I Trust God's Promise

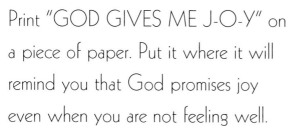

Print "GOD GIVES ME J-O-Y" on
a piece of paper. Put it where it will
remind you that God promises joy
even when you are not feeling well.

God's Kindness

God is kind.

He promises he will be slow to get angry and he will not turn away from you when you are sorry. You don't have to be afraid to tell God the truth!

"I am the Lord, the Lord. I am a God who is tender and kind.
I am gracious. I am slow to get angry.
I am faithful and full of love."

Exodus 34:6

The Lord is gracious. He is kind and tender.
He is slow to get angry. He is full of love.

Psalm 145:8

The Lord your God is kind and tender.
He won't turn away from you if you return to him.

2 Chronicles 30:9

I Trust God's Promise

Has a friend ever turned away from you? That was unkind. But God will never do that. Try to remember if you have ever turned away from a friend. Ask God and that friend to forgive you.

God's Kindness

God showed his promise to be kind
when Jesus welcomed children to talk to him
instead of only talking to grown-ups.
God is kind to promise he will always
listen to you—not just to grown-ups.

(God said) "You will come and pray to me.
And I will listen to you."

Jeremiah 29:12

Jesus said, "Let the little children come to me.
Don't keep them away. The kingdom of heaven
belongs to people like them."

Matthew 19:14

Then (Jesus) took the children in his arms.
He put his hands on them and blessed them.

Mark 10:16

I Trust God's Promise

Can you imagine being one of the girls
Jesus listened to when he was on earth?
Dress up like a girl from Bible times. Thank
God for his promise to listen to all his
children—including you!

God's Love

The Bible tells you that God is love.

God loves you so much that he chose you
and promises that the two of you will always
be together when you love him too.
God and you—what a team!

God is love. Anyone who leads a life of love shows
that he is joined to God. And God is joined to him.

1 John 4:16

The Lord loves you. God chose you from the beginning.

2 Thessalonians 2:13

The Lord loves us very much …
His loving concern never fails.
His great love is new every morning.

Lamentations 3:22–23

I Trust God's Promise

When you have a partner at school or in a game, you should work as a team and both do your best. God does his best for you every day. Name three ways you can do your best for God. (Hint: Help others.)

God's Love

God loves you so much

that he promised to send Jesus to take
the punishment for your wrongs.
Because when Jesus was born God kept that
promise, you can live with him in heaven someday.

How did God show his love for us?
He sent his one and only Son into the world.
He sent him so we could receive life through him.

1 John 4:9

(Jesus said) "God loved the world so much that he gave
his one and only Son. Anyone who believes in him
will not die but will have eternal life."

John 3:16

Nothing at all can ever separate us from God's love
because of what Christ Jesus our Lord has done.

Romans 8:39

I Trust God's Promise

Name three things about you that people didn't know when you were born.

Now name three things most people did not know about Jesus when he was born. (Hint: He connects us to God.)

God's Miracles

God shows his promises through his great miracles—like when he promised to save Daniel from the lions' den, and he did it! All of his miracles make a promise that says he is the one, true, miracle-making God.

He does miraculous signs and wonders.
He does them in the heavens and on the earth.
He has saved Daniel from the power of the lions.

Daniel 6:27

The Lord will command his angels to take good care of you.

Psalm 91:11

The Lord showed you those things
so that you might know he is God.
There is no other God except him.

Deuteronomy 4:35

I Trust God's Promise

God protects people every day better
than people can protect themselves—from
accidents or from others who might hurt
them. Is God protecting you today?
Remember, sometimes he sends angels!

God's Miracles

Everything about Jesus

is a promised miracle: God is his father.

He did miracles while he was on earth.

And after Jesus died for you, he came alive again

so you can have the miracle of eternal life.

Can you say "Wow!"?

"The Lord himself will give you a miraculous sign.
The virgin is going to have a baby. She will give birth to a son.
And he will be called Immanuel."

Isaiah 7:14

The people saw the miraculous sign that Jesus did.
Then they began to say, "This must be the Prophet
who is supposed to come into the world."

John 6:14

Jesus is not here! He has risen!
Remember how he told you he would rise.

Luke 24:6

I Trust God's Promise

Jesus said he would die and then come back
to life on earth. He did it just as he promised!
Now you can live in heaven someday. If you
are where it is okay to make noise, shout,
"It's a miracle!"

God's Patience

God showed his promise to be patient
in many ways. He was patient while he waited
for people to decide to board Noah's boat.
He gave Jonah time in the fish to decide to obey him.
And Jesus is patient about returning to earth
so we all have time to decide to follow him.

God was patient while Noah was building the ark.

1 Peter 3:20

From inside the fish Jonah prayed to the Lord his God.

Jonah 2:1-2

The Lord … is patient with you …
Remember that while our Lord is waiting patiently to return,
people are being saved.

2 Peter 3:9, 15

I Trust God's Promise

Answer some questions about Jonah's story (JONAH 1-3): What did Jonah do instead of going to Nineveh? What swallowed Jonah and then spit him out? How long was Jonah in there before he decided to do what was right?

God's Peace

God promises to bless you with peace.

When you have peace, you can rest.
When you rest, you have more strength
to do what is right. When you do right
and are faithful to God,
he keeps blessing you with peace.

I will listen to what God the Lord will say.
He promises peace to his faithful people.

Psalm 85:8

The Lord gave them peace and rest on every side.
That's what he had promised their fathers he would do.

Joshua 21:44

The Lord blesses his people with peace.

Psalm 29:11

I Trust God's Promise

See the butterflies on this page? They seem peaceful, don't they? Sometimes they fly around, and sometimes they land on a flower or someone's hand. Tell how people can be peaceful. (Hint: They don't argue.)

God's Peace

Sometimes you are worried

or troubled, right? That's when God really shows his
promise to give you peace. He says not to worry or
be afraid. He even promises to make your enemies
live in peace with you when you live for him!

Don't worry about anything. Instead, tell God about everything.
Ask and pray. Give thanks to him. Then God's peace will watch over
your hearts and your minds because you belong to Christ Jesus.

Philippians 4:6–7

(Jesus said) "I leave my peace with you. I give my peace to you …
Do not let your hearts be troubled. And do not be afraid."

John 14:27

When the way you live pleases the Lord,
he makes even your enemies live at peace with you.

Proverbs 16:7

I Trust God's Promise

God promises you can tell him all about what worries or troubles you. He will work to bring peace to your heart and to everyone around you too. Tell God about any trouble now. Then believe he will bring you peace.

God's Power

God has great power.

He promises to do more than you can ever imagine or ask for. He promises to use his power to save you from trouble. And God promises to give you power and love to control yourself and do what is right. Now that's power!

God is able to do far more than we could ever ask for or imagine.
He does everything by his power that is working in us.

Ephesians 3:20

Anyone who does what is right may have many troubles.
But the Lord saves him from all of them.

Psalm 34:19

(God) gave us a spirit that gives us power and love. It helps us control ourselves.

2 Timothy 1:7

I Trust God's Promise

A strong weight lifter can hold his heavy weights high above his head for a little while. That's amazing! But God promises he is always using his power for us. Name three ways he does this. (Hint: Controlling our tongues.)

God's Power

You can ask God to use his power

to help you. He promises he will do it when
you believe in his power and call out to him.
God also gives you what you need when you
and other believers ask him together.

(The Lord said) "Call out to me when trouble comes.
I will save you. And you will honor me."

Psalm 50:15

(Jesus said) "If you believe,
you will receive what you ask for when you pray."

Matthew 21:22

When you come together in the name of our Lord Jesus …
the power of our Lord Jesus will also be with you.

1 Corinthians 5:4

I Trust God's Promise

Name three kinds of people who are strong.
(Hint: A fast swimmer.) Being strong allows
people to do amazing things. But no one has
the same strong power God has. And he
promises to use his power for us.

God's Protection

God promises to watch out for you,
to keep you away from harm, and especially to watch
out for Satan. One way for you to keep trouble far
away is by obeying the Ten Commandments
God gave Moses (Exodus 20).
He gave them to help protect you from trouble!

The Lord will keep you from every kind of harm.
He will watch over your life.

Psalm 121:7

But the Lord is faithful. He will strengthen you.
He will guard you from the evil one.

2 Thessalonians 3:3

But for all time to come I show love
to all those who love me and keep my commandments.

Deuteronomy 5:10

I Trust God's Promise

One of God's Ten Commandments says to honor your father and mother. This includes anyone who is like a parent to you and who cares for you. Name three ways you can honor someone. (Hint: Only say nice things about them.)

God's Protection

God promises to protect you

by making himself a safe place. It's like he has big arms to wrap around you or big wings to spread over you. Be sure to remember that he is your safe place when trouble comes.

You can run to (God) for safety.
His powerful arms are always there to carry you.

Deuteronomy 33:27

(God) will cover you with his wings.
Under the feathers of his wings you will find safety.
He is faithful. He will keep you safe like a shield or a tower.

Psalm 91:4

God is our place of safety. He gives us strength.
He is always there to help us in times of trouble.

Psalm 46:1

I Trust God's Promise

See how God parted the sea to help people escape the soldiers chasing them back in Moses' time? After that, the waters went back together and trapped the soldiers when God told Moses to hold out his hand. Tell how God keeps you safe.

God's Rewards

Do you like rewards?

God promises to give you rewards when you belong to him and live the way he wants you to. But his Word says that you must believe in him and his promise first. Do you believe?

Good men will receive rewards for how they've lived.

Proverbs 14:14

(Jesus said) "Look! I am coming soon! I bring my rewards with me. I will reward each person for what he has done."

Revelation 22:12

Without faith it isn't possible to please God. Those who come to God must believe that he exists. And they must believe that he rewards those who look to him.

Hebrews 11:6

I Trust God's Promise

Guess what the Bible says? "Children are a gift from the Lord. They are a reward from him" (Psalm 127:3). Think about some of the friends you love and thank God for them.

God's Rewards

God promises rewards

when you work for him and do what is right. Some rewards come on earth, like success at what God wants you to do. Some rewards will come to you in heaven, like a special room Jesus will prepare just for you—his daughter!

Work because you know that you will finally receive as a reward what the Lord wants you to have.
You are serving the Lord Christ.
Colossians 3:24

Success is the reward of those who do right.
Proverbs 13:21

(Jesus said) "There are many rooms in my Father's house. If this were not true, I would have told you. I am going there to prepare a place for you."
John 14:2

I Trust God's Promise

Do you have a special room, or corner, or tree house? No matter how special it is, it can't compare to the room you'll have in heaven. Draw a picture of the kind of room you would like in heaven.

God's Son, Jesus

The plan God promised to save us

was all worked out long before Jesus came
to earth. He planned for Jesus' birth, his death,
his resurrection, and his work.

What a planner God is!

"Today in the town of David a Savior has been born to you.
He is Christ the Lord."

Luke 2:11

Jesus has been given a greater work to do for God.

Hebrews 8:6

He took the sins of many people on himself.
And he gave his life for those who had done what is wrong.

Isaiah 53:12

I Trust God's Promise

God made plans for Jesus and he makes plans for us—good plans. Tell what you think some of God's plans might be for you. (Hint: To believe in Jesus.)

God's Son, Jesus

God's promise in Jesus

is that Jesus makes it possible for you to be
with God forever. If you believe Jesus is alive
and went back to heaven, then you will be saved.
You will live in heaven someday forever.

(Jesus said) "Before long, the world will not see me anymore.
But you will see me. Because I live, you will live also."

John 14:19

Jesus said … "I am the resurrection and the life.
Anyone who believes in me will live, even if he dies."

John 11:25

Say with your mouth, "Jesus is Lord."
Believe in your heart that God raised him from the dead.
Then you will be saved.

Romans 10:9

I Trust God's Promise

Say this aloud: "Jesus is Lord!" Now say, "Jesus is my Lord!" Now say, "Jesus can be everyone's Lord!" Do you believe it? Who can you tell about Jesus? They will want to know!

God's Son, Jesus

Many of God's promises came true because of Jesus. Jesus is like a light to show you where to find God. And you won't have to be hungry or thirsty for God because Jesus is like food and water for you.

God has made a great many promises.
They are all "Yes" because of what Christ has done.

2 Corinthians 1:20

(Jesus) said, "I am the light of the world.
Those who follow me will never walk in darkness.
They will have the light that leads to life."

John 8:12

Then Jesus said, "I am the bread of life.
No one who comes to me will ever go hungry.
And no one who believes in me will ever be thirsty."

John 6:35

I Trust God's Promise

Because of Jesus, all of God's Bible promises are true. Go into a dark closet and close the door—just for a second. Then open it again and see the light. That's what it is like with Jesus—you can see God's promises!

God's Truth

God promises he will always tell the truth.

He cannot lie because he is only good!
And God promises that his truth will not be
hard to understand. God and Jesus bless you
with grace, mercy, and peace
when you love the truth!

"I am the Lord. I always speak the truth.
I always say what is right."

Isaiah 45:19

The truth about God is plain to them. God has made it plain.

Romans 1:19

God the Father and Jesus Christ his Son will give you
grace, mercy and peace. Those blessings will be with us
because we love the truth.

2 John 1:3

I Trust God's Promise

You might want to tell a lie to get your way or keep from being corrected. But telling the truth is always God's best plan. Promise God now that you will always try to tell the whole truth!

God's Truth

God promises you can find the truth about how to live in his Word by knowing Jesus. Jesus promises you will know the truth when you follow him. Jesus' truth will keep you from being confused, uncertain, or worried.

I will guide you and teach you the way you should go.
I will give you good advice and watch over you.

Psalm 32:8

Jesus answered, "I am the way and the truth and the life."

John 14:6

"If you obey my teaching," he said, "you are really my disciples.
Then you will know the truth.
And the truth will set you free."

John 8:31–32

I Trust God's Promise

If you keep a secret about something you did wrong, then you are not free from worry. You will always be worried someone will find out. Ask God to help you tell the truth.

God's Wisdom

God promises he will give you his wisdom if you ask him. Then you will know the best thing to do. You can have knowledge, wisdom—and happiness— when you please God!

If any of you need wisdom, ask God for it.
He will give it to you.

James 1:5

I will give you words of wisdom. None of your enemies
will be able to withstand them or oppose them.

Luke 21:15

God gives wisdom, knowledge and happiness
to a man who pleases him.

Ecclesiastes 2:26

I Trust God's Promise

You can know the stove is hot, but you are wise not to touch it. That wisdom comes with learning that a hot stove can burn you. Name three wise things God can teach you. (Hint: To be truthful.)

God's Witnesses

God shows his promises through people

and his Word—his witnesses!

Jesus' followers witnessed—or saw—

Jesus alive after he died so they could tell others.

People are called to speak for or witness for Christ.

And God's Word tells everyone all about him.

(Peter said) God has raised this same Jesus back to life.
We are all witnesses of this.

Acts 2:31–32

(Jesus said)
"You will be brought to governors and kings because of me.
You will be witnesses to them ..."

Matthew 10:18

"The Scriptures you study give witness about me."

John 5:39

I Trust God's Promise

You can be a witness for God and Jesus
by telling everyone about him and by
learning Scripture. Learn John 5:39 by heart.
Say it every day this week to remind you to
love God's Word.

You, His Daughter

God is your heavenly Father.

He promises that when you obey him, others will praise him. It shows you really believe in his Son, Jesus. You can help God show his wonderful promises! Yes, YOU—his daughter!

"I will be your Father. You will be my sons and daughters, says the Lord who rules over all."

2 Corinthians 6:18

People will praise God because you obey him. That proves that you really believe the good news about Christ.

2 Corinthians 9:13